Sentenced to Life

ALSO BY CLIVE JAMES

AUTOBIOGRAPHY

Unreliable Memoirs   *Falling Towards England*
May Week Was In June   *North Face of Soho*
The Blaze of Obscurity

FICTION

Brilliant Creatures   *The Remake*
Brrm! Brrm!   *The Silver Castle*

VERSE

Other Passports: Poems 1958–1985
The Book of My Enemy: Collected Verse 1958–2003
Opal Sunset: Selected Poems 1958–2008
Angels Over Elsinore: Collected Verse 2003–2008
Nefertiti in the Flak Tower

TRANSLATION

The Divine Comedy

CRITICISM

The Metropolitan Critic (new edition, 1994)
Visions Before Midnight   *The Crystal Bucket*
First Reactions (US)   *From the Land of Shadows*
Glued to the Box   *Snakecharmers in Texas*
The Dreaming Swimmer   *Fame in the Twentieth Century*
On Television   *Even As We Speak*   *Reliable Essays*
As of This Writing (US)   *The Meaning of Recognition*
Cultural Amnesia   *The Revolt of the Pendulum*
A Point of View   *Poetry Notebook*

TRAVEL

Flying Visits

CLIVE JAMES

Sentenced to Life

POEMS 2011–2014

PICADOR

First published 2015 by Picador
an imprint of Pan Macmillan
20 New Wharf Road, London N1 9RR
Associated companies throughout the world
www.panmacmillan.com

ISBN 978-1-4472-8404-8

A CIP catalogue record for this book is available from the British Library.

Printed and bound by CPI Group (UK) Ltd, Croydon, CR0 4YY

to Prue

If you're the dreamer, I'm your dream, but when
You wish to wake I am your wish, and grow
As mighty as all mastery, and then
As silent as a star
Ablaze above the city that we know
As Time: so very strange, so very far.

Acknowledgements

I should thank Prue Shaw, Deirdre Serjeantson, Tom Stoppard, David Free and Stephen Edgar for reading these poems as they came out, and for saying what they thought. As in my two previous collections, Don Paterson helped me choose the order and bring the manuscript to a workable finality. I owe special thanks to my elder daughter Claerwen for planting the Japanese maple tree in my garden. As for my younger daughter and my entire family, and for how they looked after me at this fragile yet busy time, I lack the words to thank them sufficiently, except to say that the words might be somewhere in this little book; too much decked out with the trappings of premature sorrow, perhaps; but any strength of form is surely a reflection of how well I was guarded against despair by the joy and kindness with which I was surrounded. As often happens with poetry, the ostensible meaning and the deeper meaning might be at variance. To put it less grandly, you can say that you're on your last legs, but the way you say it might equally suggest that you could run a mile in your socks.

There are editors and poetry editors to thank: of the *New Yorker*, the *Yale Review*, the *New Statesman*, the *Spectator*, *Standpoint*, *Quadrant*, the *Australian* and the *British Medical Journal: Supportive and Palliative Care*. But above all other editors I must thank Alan Jenkins of the *TLS*, who encouraged me in the notion that a poet who is up against it might well make a subject out of being up against it. At my base in Cambridge, Susie Young and Dawn Crow combined their efforts to guide a stream of electronic manuscripts into my website and out again. I should also thank the editors and anchor-persons of various radio and television stations in the UK, Ireland, Australia and Canada who kindly asked me to read some of these poems aloud: an offence, perhaps, to those who believe that a poem should be merely overheard, but an unbeatable way of barking for one's act.

Contents

Sentenced to Life

Sentenced to Life

Sentenced to life, I sleep face-up as though
Ice-bound, lest I should cough the night away,
And when I walk the mile to town, I show
The right technique for wading through deep clay.
A sad man, sorrier than he can say.

But surely not so guilty he should die
Each day from knowing that his race is run:
My sin was to be faithless. I would lie
As if I could be true to everyone
At once, and all the damage that was done

Was in the name of love, or so I thought.
I might have met my death believing this,
But no, there was a lesson to be taught.
Now, not just old, but ill, with much amiss,
I see things with a whole new emphasis.

My daughter's garden has a goldfish pool
With six fish, each a little finger long.
I stand and watch them following their rule
Of never touching, never going wrong:
Trajectories as perfect as plain song.

Once, I would not have noticed; nor have known
The name for Japanese anemones,
So pale, so frail. But now I catch the tone
Of leaves. No birds can touch down in the trees
Without my seeing them. I count the bees.

Even my memories are clearly seen:
Whence comes the answer if I'm told I must
Be aching for my homeland. Had I been
Dulled in the brain to match my lungs of dust
There'd be no recollection I could trust.

Yet I, despite my guilt, despite my grief,
Watch the Pacific sunset, heaven sent,
In glowing colours and in sharp relief,
Painting the white clouds when the day is spent,
As if it were my will and testament –

As if my first impressions were my last,
And time had only made them more defined,
Now I am weak. The sky is overcast
Here in the English autumn, but my mind
Basks in the light I never left behind.

Driftwood Houses

The *ne plus ultra* of our lying down,
Skeleton riders see the planet peeled
Into their helmets by a knife of light.
Just so, I stare into the racing field
Of ice as I lie on my side and fight
To cough up muck. This bumpy slide downhill
Leads from my bed to where I'm bound to drown
At this rate. I get up and take a walk,
Lean on the balustrade and breathe my fill
At last. The wooden stairs down to the hall
Stop shaking. Enough said. To hear me talk
You'd think I found my fate sad. Hardly that:
All that has happened is I've hit the wall.
Disintegration is appropriate,

As once, on our French beach, I built, each year,
Among the rocks below the esplanade,
Houses from driftwood for our girls to roof
With towels so they could hide there in the shade
With ice creams that would melt more slowly. Proof
That nothing built can be forever here
Lay in the way those frail and crooked frames
Were undone by a storm-enhanced high tide
And vanished. It was time, and anyhow
Our daughters were not short of other games
Which were all theirs, and not geared to my pride.
And here they come. They're gathering shells again.
And you in your straw hat, I see you now,
As I lie restless yet most blessed of men.

Landfall

Hard to believe, now, that I once was free
From pills in heaps, blood tests, X-rays and scans.
No pipes or tubes. At perfect liberty,
I stained my diary with travel plans.

The ticket paid for at the other end,
I packed a hold-all and went anywhere
They asked me. One on whom you could depend
To show up, I would cross the world by air

And come down neatly in some crowded hall.
I stood for a full hour to give my spiel.
Here, I might talk back to a nuisance call,
And that's my flight of eloquence. Unreal:

But those years in the clear, how real were they,
When all the sirens in the signing queue
Who clutched their hearts at what I had to say
Were just dreams, even when the dream came true?

I called it health but never stopped to think
It might have been a kind of weightlessness,
That footloose feeling always on the brink
Of breakdown: the false freedom of excess.

Rarely at home in those days, I'm home now,
Where few will look at me with shining eyes.
Perhaps none ever did, and that was how
The fantasy of young strength that now dies

Expressed itself. The face that smiled at mine
Out of the looking glass was seeing things.
Today I am restored by my decline
And by the harsh awakening it brings.

I was born weak and always have been weak.
I came home and was taken into care.
A cot-case, but at long last I can speak:
I am here now, who was hardly even there.

Early to Bed

Old age is not my problem. Bad health, yes.
If I were well again, I'd walk for miles,
My name a synonym for tirelessness.
On Friday nights I'd go out on the tiles:

I'd go to tango joints and stand up straight
While women leaned against me trustingly,
I'd push them backward at a stately rate
With steps of eloquence and intricacy.

Alone in the café, my favourite place,
I'd sit up late to carve a verse like this.
I couldn't do it at my usual pace
But weight of manner would add emphasis.

The grand old man. Do I dare play that part?
Perhaps I am too frail. I don't know how
To say exactly what is in my heart,
Except I feel that I am nowhere now.

But I have tempted providence too long:
It gives me life enough, and little pain.
I should be grateful for this simple song,
No matter how it goes against the grain

To spend the best part of a winter's day
Filing away at some reluctant rhyme
And go to bed with so much still to say
On how I came to have so little time.

My Home

Grasping at straws, I bless another day
Of having felt not much less than all right.
I wrote a paragraph and put some more
Books in a box for books to throw away.
Such were my deeds. Now, short of breath and sore
From all that effort, I prepare for night,
Which occupies the windows as I climb
The stairs. A step up and I stand, each time,

Posed like the statue of a man in pain,
Although I'm really not: just weak and slow.
This is the measure of my dying years:
The sad skirl of a piper in the rain
Who plays 'My Home'. If I seem close to tears
It's for my sins, not sickness. Soon the snow
Will finish readying the ground for spring.
The cold, if not the warmth that it will bring,

Is made, each day, so clearly manifest
I thank my lucky stars for second sight.
The children of our street head off for school
Most mornings, stronger for their hours of rest.
Plump in their coloured coats they prove a rule
By moving brilliantly through soft white light:
We fade away, but vivid in our eyes
A world is born again that never dies.

Holding Court

Retreating from the world, all I can do
Is build a new world, one demanding less
Acute assessments. Too deaf to keep pace
With conversation, I don't try to guess
At meanings, or unpack a stroke of wit,
But just send silent signals with my face
That claim I've not succumbed to loneliness
And might be ready to come in on cue.
People still turn towards me where I sit.

I used to notice everything, and spoke
A language full of details that I'd seen,
And people were amused; but now I see
Only a little way. What can they mean,
My phrases? They come drifting like the mist
I look through if someone appears to be
Smiling in my direction. Have they been?
This was the time when I most liked to smoke.
My watch-band feels too loose around my wrist.

My body, sensitive in every way
Save one, can still proceed from chair to chair,
But in my mind the fires are dying fast.
Breathe through a scarf. Steer clear of the cold air.
Think less of love and all that you have lost.
You have no future so forget the past.
Let this be no occasion for despair.
Cherish the prison of your waning day.
Remember liberty, and what it cost.

Be pleased that things are simple now, at least,
As certitude succeeds bewilderment.
The storm blew out and this is the dead calm.
The pain is going where the passion went.
Few things will move you now to lose your head
And you can cause, or be caused, little harm.
Tonight you leave your audience content:
You were the ghost they wanted at the feast,
Though none of them recalls a word you said.

Procedure for Disposal

It may not come to this, but if I should
Fail to survive this year of feebleness
Which irks me so and may have killed for good
Whatever gift I had for quick success –
For I could talk an hour alone on stage
And mostly make it up along the way,
But now when I compose a single page
Of double-spaced it takes me half the day –
If I, that is, should finally succumb
To these infirmities I'm slow to learn
The names of lest my brain be rendered numb
With boredom even as I toss and turn,
Then send my ashes home, where they can fall
In their own sweet time from the harbour wall.

Manly Ferry

Too frail to fly, I may not see again
The harbour that I crossed on the *South Steyne*
When I was still in short pants. All the boys
Would gather at the rail that ran around
The open engine-room. The oil, the noise
Of rocking beams and plunging rods: it beat
Even the view out from the hurdling deck
Into the ocean. The machinery
Was so alive, so beautiful, so neat.

Years later the old ferries disappeared,
Except for the *South Steyne*, which looked intact
Where she was parked at Pyrmont, though a fire
Had gutted her. I loved her two-faced grace:
Twin funnels, and each end of her a prow,
She sailed into a mirror and back out,
Even while dead inside and standing still:
Her livery of green and gold wore well
Through years of weather as she went nowhere
Except on that long voyage in my mind
Where complicated workings clicked and throbbed
And everything moved forward at full strength.

And then, while I was elsewhere, she was gone:
And now I, too, await my vanishing,
Which, unlike hers, will be for good. She went
Away to be refitted. In her new
Career as a floating restaurant
She seems set for as long as oysters grow
With chilled white Cloudy Bay to wash them down:

A brilliant inner city ornament.
But is it better to be always there
Than out of it, and just a fading name?
For me, her life was when the engine turned.
Soon now my path across the swell will end.
If I can't work, let me be broken up.

Tempe Dump

I always thought the showdown would be sudden,
Convulsive as a bushfire triple-jumping
A roadway where some idiot Green council
Had forbidden the felling of gum trees,
And so, with no firebreaks to check its course,
The fire rides on like the army of Attila
To look for houses where the English Garden
Is banned, and there is only the Australian garden,
With eucalypts that overhang the eaves
And shed bark to ensure the racing flames
Will send the place up like a napalm strike.

Instead, it's Tempe Dump. When we were small
My gang went there exploring. Piston rings
Lay round in heaps, shiny among the junk
Which didn't shine at all, just gave forth wisps
Of smoke. The dump was smouldering underneath
But had no end in view. This is the fire
Within me, though I harbour noble thoughts
Of forests under phosphorous attack
And in an hour left black, in fields of ash –
Not this long meltdown with its leaking heat,
Its drips of acid, pools of alkali:
This slow burn of what should be finished with
But waits for the clean sweep that never comes.

Living Doll

An *Aufstehpuppe* is a stand-up guy.
You knock him over, he gets up again:
Constantly smiling, never asking why
The world went sideways for a while back then.

I have an *Aufstehpuppe* on the shelf
Under the mirror in my living room:
I wish I were reminded of myself
Merrily dipping in and out of doom.

The truth, alas, is I've been knocked askew
For quite a while now and I can't get back
To find the easy balance I once knew.
Until the day when everything goes black

I'll spend more time than he does on my side
Wishing the sparkle of his painted eyes
Was shared by mine. I envy him his pride:
That simple strength he seems to realise.

My *Aufstehpuppe* was a crude antique
When first I met him. Soon he might descend
Further into our family, there to speak
Of how we are defeated in the end,

But still begin again in the new lives
Which sort our junk, deciding what to keep.
Let them keep this, a cheap doll that contrives
To stand straight even as I fall asleep.

Event Horizon

For years we fooled ourselves. Now we can tell
How everyone our age heads for the brink
Where they are drawn into the unplumbed well,
Not to be seen again. How sad, to think
People we once loved will be with us there
And we not touch them, for it is nowhere.

Never to taste again her pretty mouth!
It's been forever, though, since last we kissed.
Shadows evaporate as they go south,
Torn, by whatever longings still persist,
Into a tattered wisp, a streak of air,
And then not even that. They get nowhere.

But once inside, you will have no regrets.
You go where no one will remember you.
You go below the sun when the sun sets,
And there is nobody you ever knew
Still visible, nor even the most rare
Hint of a face to humanise nowhere.

Are you to welcome this? It welcomes you.
The only blessing of the void to come
Is that you can relax. Nothing to do,
No cruel dreams of subtracting from your sum
Of follies. About those, at last, you care:
But soon you need not, as you go nowhere.

Into the singularity we fly
After a stretch of time in which we leave
Our lives behind yet know that we will die
At any moment now. A pause to grieve,
Burned by the starlight of our lives laid bare,
And then no sound, no sight, no thought. Nowhere.

What is it worth, then, this insane last phase
When everything about you goes downhill?
This much: you get to see the cosmos blaze
And feel its grandeur, even against your will,
As it reminds you, just by being there,
That it is here we live or else nowhere.

Nature Programme

The female panda is on heat
For about five minutes a year
And the male, no sprinter at the best of times,
Hardly ever gets there
Before she cools off again.

In the South Island of New Zealand
There is a rain forest
With penguins in it.
They trot along the dangerous trails
Towards the booming ocean

Where albatross chicks in training
For their very first take-off
Are snatched by tiger sharks
Cruising in water
No deeper than your thighs.

Doomed to the atrophy of lust,
Lurching with their flippers out,
Dragged under as they strain for flight,
They could be you:
Wonder of nature that you were.

Managing Anger

On screen, the actor smashes down the phone.
He wrecks the thing because he can't get through.
He plays it stagey even when alone.
If you were there, he might be wrecking you.

Actors believe they have to show, not tell,
Any annoyance that the script dictates,
Therefore it's not enough for them to yell:
They must pull down a cupboard full of plates.

An actor wrecks a room. The actress who
Is playing wife to him does not protest.
Perhaps she doesn't have enough to do
All day, and thinks his outburst for the best.

For God forbid that actors bottle up
Their subterranean feelings so that we
Can't see them. We must watch the coffee cup
Reduced to smithereens, the shelf swept free

Of all its crockery. Another take
Requires the whole set to be dressed again
With all the gubbins that he got to break
The first time. Aren't they weary, now and then,

The poor crew, setting up the stuff once more
That some big baby trashes in a rage,
And all that fury faked? False to the core,
The screen experience gives us a gauge

For our real lives, where we go on for years
Not even mentioning some simple fact
That brings us to the aching point of tears –
Lest people think that it might be an act.

Echo Point

I am the echo of the man you knew.
Launched from the look-out to the other side
Of this blue valley, my voice calls to you
All on its own, and more direct for that.
My line of sweet talk you could not abide
Came from the real man. It will all be gone –
Like glitter back to the magician's hat –
Soon now, and only sad scraps will remain.
His body that betrayed you has gone on
To do the same for him. Like veils of rain,
He is the cloud that his tears travel through.

When the cloud lifts, he will be gone indeed.
Hearing his cry, you'll see the ghost gums break
Into clear air, as all the past is freed
From false hopes. No, I nowhere lie awake
To feel this happen, but I know it will.
At the last breath, my throat was full of song;
The proof, for a short while, is with you still.
Though snapped at sharply by the whip-bird's call,
It has not stopped. It lingers for your sake:
Almost as if I were not gone for long –
And what you hear will not fade as I fall.

Too Much Light

My cataracts invest the bright spring day
With extra glory, with a glow that stings.
The shimmering shields above the college gates –
Heraldic remnants of the queens and kings –
Flaunt liquid paint here at the end of things
When my vitality at last abates,
And all these forms bleed, spread and make a blur
Of what, to second sight, they are and were.

And now I slowly pace, a stricken beast,
Across a lawn which must be half immersed
In crocuses and daffodils, but I
Can only see for sure the colours burst
And coalesce as if they were the first
Flowers I ever saw. Thus, should I die,
I'll go back through the gate I entered when
My eyes were stunned, as now they are again.

My Latest Fever

My latest fever clad me in cold sweat
And there I was, in hospital again,
Drenched, and expecting an attack of bugs
As devastating as the first few hours
Of *Barbarossa*, with the Russian air force
Caught on the ground and soldiers by the thousand
Herded away to starve, while Stalin still
Believed it couldn't happen. But instead
The assault turned out to be as deadly dull
As a bunch of ancient members of the Garrick
Emerging from their hutch below the stairs
To bore me from all angles as I prayed
For sleep, which only came in fits and starts.
Night after night was like that. Every day
Was like the night before, a hit parade
Of jazzed-up sequences from action movies.
While liquid drugs were pumped into my wrist,
My temperature stayed sky high. On the screen
Deep in my head, heroes repaired themselves.
In *Rambo First Blood*, Sly Stallone sewed up
His own arm. Then Mark Wahlberg, star of *Shooter*,
Assisted by Kate Mara, operated
To dig the bullets from his body. Teeth
Were gritted in both cases. No-one grits
Like Sly: it looks like a piano sneering.
Better, however, to be proof against
All damage, as in *Salt*, where Angelina
Jumps from a bridge onto a speeding truck
And then from that truck to another truck.
In North Korea, tortured for years on end,

She comes out with a split lip. All this mayhem
Raged in my brain with not a cliché scamped.
I saw the heroes march in line towards me
In slow-mo, with a wall of flame behind them,
And thought, as I have often thought, 'This is
The pits. How can I make it stop?' It stopped.
On the eleventh day, my temperature
Dived off the bridge like Catherine Zeta-Jones
From the Petronas towers in Kuala Lumpur.
I had no vision of the final battle.
The drugs, in pill form now, drove back the bugs
Into the holes from which they had attacked.
It might have been a scene from *Starship Troopers*:
But no, I had returned to the real world.
They sent me home to sleep in a dry bed
Where I felt better than I had for months.
No need to make a drama of my rescue:
Having been saved was like a lease of life,
The thing itself, undimmed by images –
A thrill a minute simply for being so.

The Emperor's Last Words

An army that never leaves its defences
Is bound to be defeated, said Napoleon,
Who left them, and was defeated.
And thus I gather my remaining senses
For the walk, or limp, to town
Where I have a haircut and visit
The Oxfam bookshop near the bridge.

Only a day out of Addenbrooke's
Where another bout of pneumonia
Damned near nailed me,
I walk slowly now, sitting on low brick walls.
But the haircut is successful,
Completing my resemblance to Buzz Aldrin
On the surface of Jupiter,

And in the bookshop I get, for my niece,
The Penguin Book of English Verse
(John Hayward's excellent anthology)
And the old, neat, thin-paper OUP edition
Of the Louise and Aylmer Maude translation
Of *War and Peace*, so handy for the pocket.

Still in her teens, already reading everything,
She wants to be a writer, and when she visits me
She gets a useful lesson
On how a writer can end up.
But things could have been worse:
I could have been married to Laura Riding,
Whose collected poems I purchase for myself.
Have fifteen years of death improved her verses?

No, still stridently incomprehensible, befitting
The way she won an argument with Robert Graves
By throwing herself backwards from a window:
A token, no doubt, of an artistic commitment
The purity of whose achievements was proved
By being intelligible to nobody at all
Except her fellow fruit-cakes.

Well, she sure left her defences.
Almost everyone wants to be a writer.
My niece, however, has got the knack:
That feeling for a sentence, you can't mistake it.
The only question is how far you will go,
Even walking ever so slowly,
Away from your fortress. All the way to Russia?

But Tolstoy, himself an awful husband,
Waits to make a midget of your memory.
You escaped from Elba
But not from St Helena.
Had you stayed in Corsica
None of this would have happened.
But you left, and now every nut ward in the world
Has one of you at least.

The Maudes were married more than fifty years.
In two days' time, the Tour de France
Will go past here
Where I now sit to gather strength
For my retreat from this hot sun.
It's time to go. High time to go. High time.
France, army, head of the army, Josephine.

Compendium Catullianum

My girlfriend's sparrow is dead. It is an ex-sparrow.
Where once it hopped about between her knees,
Today it limps along the same dark road
I've come to know too well since she denied me
The pathway to her lap. Cruel Lesbia,
You asked for this, your sparrow with its feet
Turned upwards as yours were when in the throes
Of love. If I say 'Screw it, it's just a sparrow'
I court your wrath, or, worse, your cold rejection;
But I can live with that though you weep floods,
Since I have friends who steer well clear of war.
Give me charm over courage every time:
The ease of bantering chaps, a faithful love
From women or even for them, so long as they
Don't pester me like you and your dumb sparrow.
Remember when I asked for a thousand kisses?
Let's make it ten. Why not just kiss me once?
For I, tear-drenched as when my brother died,
Miss you the way you miss that stupid bird:
Excruciating. Let's live and let's love.
Our brief light spent, night is an endless sleep.

Bugsy Siegel's Flying Eye

In Havana, at the hotel Nacional,
Lucky Luciano, or so the story goes,
Persuaded a reluctant Meyer Lansky
That Bugsy Siegel, who had squandered the mob's money
On taking years to finish the Flamingo
And might even have skimmed from the invested capital,
Would need to have his venture in Las Vegas
Brought to a sudden end.

But the execution happened in LA
With Bugsy unwisely sitting near a window.
The first bullet took out his right eye
And flung it far away across the carpet
Into the tiled dining area.
He should have known that something bad would happen
Because when he got home he had smelled flowers
And when there are no flowers in the house
But you still smell them, it means death.

After the window shattered, the smell of jasmine
Seeped through the house, but that was no premonition,
Because Bugsy was already dead.
Scholars still ask the question why
He never guessed that he would soon get hit,
Even after closing down his dream-land
For yet another re-design. He was
An artist among gangsters. The others weren't.

When I got to Vegas, the original Flamingo
Had been torn down, with a garden on the site,
But in Havana, at the Nacional,
I met the waiter who had built a long career
Out of once having slept with Ava Gardner,
And I sat to drink mojitos where Meyer Lansky
And Lucky Luciano might once have done the same
While they pondered what to do about Bugsy.
Maybe they did. It was mob business
So nothing got written down. Nobody can be sure
Of anything except that flying eye.

Only the Immortal Need Apply

'I am as the demon of the tumult'
– Gabriele d'Annunzio, quoted by Lucy Hughes-Hallett in *The Pike*

In Paris, at Diaghilev's *Cleopatra* –
Décor by Bakst, choreography by Fokine,
Ida Rubinstein in the title role –
D'Annunzio and his powerful halitosis
Sat beside Robert de Montesquieu,
The model for Proust's Baron de Charlus.

Rubinstein, who could not dance a step,
Merely stood there looking beautiful
Or adopted the occasional Egyptian pose,
While d'Annunzio laid his plans.

Backstage in her crowded dressing-room
The Nile-nymph recovered from her exertions
By lying back in her couch.
D'Annunzio was six inches shorter than she was
But her posture put him within range.

He fell to his knees and kissed her lovely legs
Upward from toes to crotch.
As he plunged his face into the *tarte tatin*,
Barrès and Rostand bowed their heads in awe
And Montesquieu adjusted his moustache.

Later on a man in the street was arrested
And charged with not being famous.
He remains nameless to this day.

Plot Points

On the rafting ice
The afterbirth of seals
Leaves stains like pink blancmange.
Glyco proteins in the fish
Keep them from freezing.

M13 in Hercules
Is a globular star cluster –
A glitterball that my mother
Could have danced the Charleston under.
She had lovely hands.

Renoir, choosing models, always looked
At their hands first.
After the war, at Lodz,
On a tour of the concentration camp,
Rubinstein said 'I was born here.'

In Melanesia, the House of Memories
Contains the treasures of the tribe.
The Somme chalk was good for tunnels.
When the barrage broke them,
The parapet bags spat white.

At Kokoda, the treetop phosphorescence
Turned the night to Christmas.
The Aussies in Tobruk
Brushed dust from bully beef.
In the dry valleys of Antarctica
Dust is raised by the katabatic wind.

With the *Wehrmacht* stalled in front of Moscow,
Even the grease froze. The 88s
Were jammed by their own shells.
Rasputitsa was the mud
Of spring thaw and autumn rain.

On a hard day in the Alhambra
The Sultan sent an apple
To the virgin of his choice.
The logo on your Macbook
Is an echo of the manner
In which Alan Turing killed himself.

In the battle for Berlin
The last panzers were overrun
Before they reached the start-line.
A dead hippo in the *Tiergarten*
Had an unexploded mortar bomb
Sticking out of its side.

While you were reading this
Millions of stars moved closer
Towards their own extinction
So many years ago –
But let's believe our eyes:
They say it's all here now.

One Elephant, Two Elephant

Denis Zafiro, Last of the Great White Hunters –
Reduced now, a fact worth blessing, to the role of guide –
No rifle any more, just a mid-range Japanese camera
And even that he would keep under wraps. 'The last
Of the great white photographers.' One of his jokes –

Took Hemingway out on the almost fatal safari
In which Papa, extravagantly even for him,
Contrived to be in a plane crash twice, thus smashing
Himself up good, so that on his epaulettes
Could be seen, Denis said, grey muck coming out of his skull
Like oatmeal porridge.

                     Last of the great white contacts,
Denis, when our safari left Nairobi
Could have ridden up front like Rommel in his staff car
Attacking out of retreat at Sidhi Barani,
But no, he stayed modestly in the background
While our cameraman, intrepid as all get out
Knocked off the required footage of lions and tigers
And cheetahs licking their lips, with even a glimpse of leopard,
Considered unfindable save by Denis's sidekick
Kungu, who muttered comments in Swahili
Which Denis translated as 'Leopard over there, I think.'

And there she was, a set of spots deep in a tree-clump
Stuck to the spot with her spots resolutely unchanging
For the full two hours till she finally took a crap.
'A bowel movement, but at least she moved' jested Denis
Who had a million of them.

So it went on:
Good usable stuff up till the day we rested
The crew, as the union dictates. Thank God for those rules
Or there would be crosses all over the Masai Mara
To mark the death by exhaustion of the modern *impi*,
The tough men in sleeveless bush shirts
With the tricep tattoos and a camera on their shoulder
That you and I could barely pick up. Our chap was Mike:
'We're doing OK so far but nothing fantastic,
So if you two see anything don't for Christ's sake tell me.'

Denis thought that an off-piste mini-safari
With me up front while Kungu taught me Swahili
And him in the back at ease like Diana Dors
In a Daimler (his showbiz images tended to be
A bit out of date, though it's never wise to argue
With a man who actually knew Ava Gardner),
A trip to show me a few unscripted attractions
That often won't sit still for a movie camera,
Would be a good thing. He was like a book collector
Showing you his library. I could tell from how he spoke
He was Africa mad, so he had his favourite locations
For shooting stills, like a ford five miles away
Of bumpy driving, nothing too bad, he promised.
And pretty, even if nothing happened. Well he
Was right, it was pretty. Just wrong about the nothing.

We stood on the inner bank of a curve in the river
And I had to take it on trust that under the surface
Was a shallow stretch the bigger beasts could walk on.

'Elephant,' he said 'quite often cross here.
You see whole families of them at a time.'
As if on cue, three elephant, four elephant,
An entire family showed up out of the bush
Which guarded the other side like a crescent moon
And assembled on the bank. 'Well, there you are'
Laughed Denis. 'Your luck's uncanny. Straight from the movies.
No wonder Kungu wants to touch you so often.'

But even as he spoke, there were lots more of them,
So the first ones had to move, like shunted box cars,
Into the oxtail water. More than thirty
Were now in the frame, except we had no frame;
But Denis's Nikon made a rare appearance.
'Well, Kungu can pick them. This is all your doing.
I've never seen this, never in all my time
In Africa. And neither has he.'

                              And Kungu was speaking:
In between the air-horn blasts from a New York gridlock
With half of downtown occupied by Mack ten-wheelers
I caught a few mentions of *tembo*, meaning elephant,
But the other words were double Dutch to me.
'He hasn't seen this since he was a boy.'
And there were more to come, but by now the Kombis
Of all the tourist firms were gathering
At the point where the first family were now emerging
To climb the bank on the side near us.

                              A lane was left
To let the elephant by, but the flashing lights
On the cameras must have seemed a storm. One tusker
Flared out its ears and bellowed. 'By Christ'

Said Denis 'If this one charges, they all will.'
They didn't charge, but there was a bit of a panic,
And that was scary enough. I know I sound
Like Falstaff telling Hal how many thieves
He put to flight, but really there were fifty
Elephant tightly packed and churning around
To take their turn at scrambling from the soup.
In the river, the tots beside their mothers
Were near invisible, their little trunks
Held up like snorkels.

                            Open mouthed
(Like the Three Stooges, Denis later said,
Bang up to date as usual. Thanks a bunch.)
We watched one hip-deep mother tuck her trunk beneath
Her pup and hoik him out, swing like a crane
And put him on the bank. And guess who didn't
Get the shot. 'Oh blast!' said Denis, fiddling
With the switches that had changed his life.

                                    Kungu
Was of the opinion that the magic touch
Was mine, but he was also the first one –
As we bumped slowly home across the veldt –
To say what needed saying. Denis said
'He says we have to keep our day a secret.'
I dumbly added 'Especially from my crew.'
'That's who he meant,' said Denis. Pale pink light
Was growing deeper in the sky
When we got back to camp. Cameraman Mike
Said 'Anything good happen?' From the way
We said it hadn't he soon guessed that it had
But kept shtum for our young producer's sake,
And anyway next day we filmed two leopard.

Asma Unpacks Her Pretty Clothes

Wherever her main residence is now,
Asma unpacks her pretty clothes.
It takes forever: so much silk and cashmere
To be unpeeled from clinging leaves of tissue
By her ladies. With her perfect hands, she helps.

Out there in Syria, the torturers
Arrive by bus at every change of shift
While victims dangle from their cracking wrists.
Beaten with iron bars, young people pray
To die soon. This is the middle ages
Brought back to living death. Her husband's doing,
The screams will never reach her where she is.

Asma's uncovered hair had promised progress
For all her nation's women. They believed her.
We who looked on believed the promise too,
But now, as she unpacks her pretty clothes,
The dream at home dissolves in agony.

Bashar, her husband, does as he sees fit
To cripple every enemy with pain.
We sort of knew, but he had seemed so modern
With Asma alongside him. His big talk
About destroying Israel: standard stuff.
A culture-changing wife offset all that.

She did, she did. I doted as *Vogue* did
On her sheer style. Dear God, it fooled me too,
So now my blood is curdled by the shrieks
Of people mad with grief. My own wrists hurt

As Asma, with her lustrous fingertips –
She must have thought such things could never happen –
Unpacks her pretty clothes.

Nina Kogan's Geometrical Heaven

Two of her little pictures grace my walls:
Suprematism in a special sense,
With all the usual bits and pieces flying
Through space, but carrying a pastel-tinged
Delicacy to lighten the strict forms
Of that hard school and blow them all sky-high,
Splinters and stoppers from the bombing of
An angel's boudoir. When Malevich told
His pupils that their personalities
Should be suppressed, the maestro little knew
The state would soon require exactly that.
But Nina, trying as she might, could not
Rein in her individuality,
And so she made these things that I own now
And gaze at, wondering at her sad fate.
She could have got away, but wished instead
Her gift devoted to Utopia.
She painted trams, designed official posters:
Alive until the siege of Leningrad
And then gone. Given any luck, she starved:
But the purges were still rolling, and I fear
The NKVD had her on a list,
And what she faced, there at the very end,
Was the white cold. Were there an afterlife,
We might meet up, and I could tell her then
Her sumptuous fragments still went flying on
In my last hours, when I, in a warm house,
Lay on my couch to watch them coming close,
Her proofs that any vision of eternity
Is with us in the world, and beautiful

Because a mind has found the way things fit
Purely by touch. That being said, however,
I should record that out of any five
Pictures by Kogan, at least six are fakes.

Star System

The stars in their magnificent array
Look down upon the Earth, their cynosure,
Or so it seems. They are too far away,
In fact, to see a thing; hence they look pure
To us. They lack the textures of our globe,
So only we, from cameras carried high,
Enjoy the beauty of the swirling robe
That wraps us up, the interplay of sky
And cloud, as if a Wedgwood plate of blue
And white should melt, and then, its surface stirred
With spoons, a treasure too good to be true,
Be placed, and hover like a hummingbird,
Drawing all eyes, though ours alone, to feast
On splendour as it turns west from the east.

There was a time when some of our young men
Walked plumply on the moon and saw Earth rise,
As stunning as the sun. The years since then
Have aged them. Now and then somebody dies.
It's like a clock, for those of us who saw
The Saturn rockets going up as if
Mankind had energy to burn. The law
Is different for one man. Time is a cliff
You come to in the dark. Though you might fall
As easily as on a feather bed,
It is a sad farewell. You loved it all.
You dream that you might keep it in your head.
But memories, where can you take them to?
Take one last look at them. They end with you.

And still the Earth revolves, and still the blaze
Of stars maintains a show of vigilance.
It should, for long ago, in olden days,
We came from there. By luck, by fate, by chance,
All of the elements that form the world
Were sent by cataclysms deep in space,
And from their combination life unfurled
And stood up straight, and wore a human face.
I still can't pass a mirror. Like a boy,
I check my looks, and now I see the shell
Of what I was. So why, then, this strange joy?
Perhaps an old man dying would do well
To smile as he rejoins the cosmic dust
Life comes from, for resign himself he must.

Change of Domicile

Installed in my last house, I face the thought
That fairly soon there will be one house more,
Lacking the pictures and the books that here
Surround me with abundant evidence
I spent a lifetime pampering my mind.
The new place will be of a different sort,
Dark and austere, and I will have to find
My way along its unforthcoming walls.
Help is at hand here should I fall, but there
There will be no-one to turn on the lights
For me, and I will know I am not blind
Only by glimpses when the empty halls
Lead me to empty rooms, in which the nights
Succeed each other with no day between.

I may not see my tattered Chinese screen
Again, but I shall have time to reflect
That what I miss was just the bric-a-brac
I kept with me to blunt my solitude,
Part of my brave face when my life was wrecked
By my gift for deceit. Truth clears away
So many souvenirs. The shelves come clean.
In the last, the truly last house there will be
No treasured smithereens to take me back
To when things hung together. I'll conclude
The way that I began so long ago:
With nothingness, but know it fit for me
This time around, now I am brought so low,
Yet ready to move soon. When, I can't say.

Rounded with a Sleep

The sun seems in control, the tide is out:
Out to the sandbar shimmers the lagoon.
The little children sprint, squat, squeal and shout.
These shallows will be here until the moon
Contrives to reassert its influence,
And anyway, by then it will be dark.
Old now and sick, I ponder the immense
Ocean upon which I will soon embark:
As if held in abeyance by dry land
It waits for me beyond that strip of sand.

It won't wait long. Just for the moment, though,
There's time to question if my present state
Of bathing in this flawless afterglow
Is something I deserve. I left it late
To come back to my family. Here they are,
Camped on their towels and putting down their books
To watch my grand-daughter, a natural star,
Cartwheel and belly-flop. The whole scene looks
As if I thought it up to soothe my soul.
But in Arcadia, Death plays a role:

A leading role, and suddenly I wake
To realise that I've been sound asleep
Here at my desk. I just wish the mistake
Were rare, and not so frequent I could weep.
The setting alters, but the show's the same:
One long finale, soaked through with regret,
Somehow designed to expiate self-blame.
But still there is no end, at least not yet:
No cure, that is, for these last years of grief
As I repent and yet find no relief.

My legs are sore, and it has gone midnight.
I've had my last of lounging on the beach
To see the sweet oncoming sunset light
Touching the water with a blush of peach,
Smoothing the surface like a ballroom floor
As all my loved ones pack up from their day
And head back up the cliff path. This for sure:
Even the memories will be washed away,
If not by waves, by rain, which I see fall,
Drenching the flagstones and the garden wall.

My double doors are largely glass. I stand
Often to contemplate the neat back yard
My elder daughter with her artist's hand
Designed for me. This winter was less hard
Than its three predecessors were. The snow
Failed to arrive this time, but rain, for me,
Will also do to register time's flow.
The rain, the snow, the inexorable sea:
I get the point. I'll climb the stairs to bed,
Perhaps to dream I'm somewhere else instead.

All day tomorrow I have tests and scans,
And everything that happens will be real.
My blood might say I should make no more plans,
And when it does so, that will be the deal.
But until then I love to speak with you
Each day we meet. Sometimes we even touch
Across the sad gulf that I brought us to.
Just for a time, so little means so much:
More than I'm worth, I know, as I know how
My death is something I must live with now.

Elementary Sonnet

Tired out from getting up and getting dressed
I lie down for a while to get some rest,
And so begins another day of not
Achieving much except to dent the cot
For just the depth appropriate to my weight –
Which is no chasm, in my present state.
By rights my feet should barely touch the floor
And yet my legs are heavy metal. More
And more I sit down to write less and less,
Taking a half hour's break from helplessness
To craft a single stanza meant to give
Thanks for the heartbeat which still lets me live:
A consolation even now, so late – ·
When soon my poor bed will be smooth and straight.

Leçons de ténèbres

But are they lessons, all these things I learn
Through being so far gone in my decline?
The wages of experience I earn
Would service well a younger life than mine.
I should have been more kind. It is my fate
To find this out, but find it out too late.

The mirror holds the ruins of my face
Roughly together, thus reminding me
I should have played it straight in every case,
Not just when forced to. Far too casually
I broke faith when it suited me, and here
I am alone, and now the end is near.

All of my life I put my labour first.
I made my mark, but left no time between
The things achieved, so, at my heedless worst,
With no life, there was nothing I could mean.
But now I have slowed down. I breathe the air
As if there were not much more of it there

And write these poems, which are funeral songs
That have been taught to me by vanished time:
Not only to enumerate my wrongs
But to pay homage to the late sublime
That comes with seeing how the years have brought
A fitting end, if not the one I sought.

Winter Plums

Two winter plum trees grow beside my door.
Throughout the cold months they had little pink
Flowers all over them as if they wore
Nightdresses, and their branches, black as ink
By sunset, looked as if a Japanese
Painter, while painting air, had painted these

Two winter plum trees. Summer now at last
Has warmed their leaves and all the blooms are gone.
A year that I might not have had has passed.
Bare branches are my signal to go on,
But soon the brave flowers of the winter plums
Will flare again, and I must take what comes:

Two winter plum trees that will outlive me.
Thriving with colour even in the snow,
They'll snatch a triumph from adversity.
All right for them, but can the same be so
For someone who, seeing their buds remade
From nothing, will be less pleased than afraid?

Spring Snow Dancer

Snow into April. Frost night after night.
Out on the Welsh farms the lambs die unborn.
The chill air hurts my lungs, but from the light
It could be spring. Bitter as it is bright,
The last trick of the cold is a false dawn.

I breathed, grew up, and now I learn to be
Glad for my long life as it melts away,
Yet still regales me with so much to see
Of how we live in continuity
And die in it. Take what I saw today:

My granddaughter, as quick as I could glance,
Did ballet steps across the kitchen floor,
And this time I was breathless at the chance
By which I'd lived to see our dear lamb dance –
Though soon I will not see her any more.

Mysterious Arrival of the Dew

Tell me about the dew. Some say it falls
But does it fall in fact? And if it fall
Then where does it fall from? And why, in falling,
Does it not obscure the moon?

Dew on the hibiscus, dew on the cobweb,
Dew on the broken leaf,
The world's supply of diamond ear-rings
Tossed from a car window.

Some intergalactic hoodlum sugar-daddy
Is trying to get girls.
Goethe had a name for these flattering droplets:
Shiver-pearls. Grab a handful.

Statistics say dew doesn't fall at all:
Going nowhere near the moon,
It just gathers on any susceptible surface
When the temperature is right.

There is talk in every arid country
Of collecting it by the truck-load,
But the schemes get forgotten in the sun
As soon as it sucks up those trillion baubles.

Tell me about the dew. Is it a case
Of falling back the better to advance,
By the same veil, shawl or glittering pashmina
As last time out? But darling, it's to die for.

Cabin Baggage

My niece is heading here to stay with us.
Before she leaves home she takes careful stock
Of what she might not know again for years.
The berries (so she writes) have been brought in,
But she'll be gone before the peaches come.
On days of burning sun, the air is tinged
With salt and eucalyptus. 'Why am I
Leaving all this behind? I feel a fool.'
But I can tell from how she writes things down
The distance will assist her memories
To take full form. She travels to stay still.
I wish I'd been that smart before I left.
Instead, I have to dig deep for a trace
Of how the beach was red hot underfoot,
The green gold of the Christmas beetle's wing.

Transit Visa

He had not thought that it would be his task
To gauge the force of the oncoming wave
Of night; to cast aside his jester's mask,
Guessing it was not Ali Baba's cave
That would engulf him, but an emptiness
Devoid of treasure heaped to serve his dreams;
His best hope, to be set free from distress.
No guiding light, not even moonlight beams,
Will lead him forward to find life refined
Into a fit reward or punishment:
No soul can well continue when the mind
Fades with the body. All his store is spent
Of pride, or guilt, or anything that might
Have steeled him for the non-stop outbound flight

Were it to lead somewhere, but it does not.
That much becomes clear as the sky grows dark.
He hears the rattle of his childhood cot,
The rain that fills the creek that floods the park:
But these are memories. The way ahead
Will send no messages that can be kept.
One doesn't even get to meet the dead.
You planned to see the bed where Dido slept?
No chance. It didn't last the course. Back then
They forged the myths that feed our poetry
Not for our sake, but theirs, to soothe them when
Life was so frightful that death had to be
A better place, a holiday from fear.
But now we know that paradise is here,

As is the underworld. To no new dawn
He gets him gone, nor yet a starry hour
Of silence. He goes back to being born
And then beyond that, though he feels the power
Of all creation when he lifts a book,
Or when a loved face smiles at his new joke,
Which could well be his last: but now just look
At how the air, before he turns to smoke,
Is glowing in the window. If the glass
Were brighter it would melt. That radiance
Is not a way of saying this will pass:
It says this will remain. No play of chance
From now on includes you. The world you quit
Is staying here, so say goodbye to it.

Japanese Maple

Your death, near now, is of an easy sort.
So slow a fading out brings no real pain.
Breath growing short
Is just uncomfortable. You feel the drain
Of energy, but thought and sight remain:

Enhanced, in fact. When did you ever see
So much sweet beauty as when fine rain falls
On that small tree
And saturates your brick back garden walls,
So many Amber Rooms and mirror halls?

Ever more lavish as the dusk descends
This glistening illuminates the air.
It never ends.
Whenever the rain comes it will be there,
Beyond my time, but now I take my share.

My daughter's choice, the maple tree is new.
Come autumn and its leaves will turn to flame.
What I must do
Is live to see that. That will end the game
For me, though life continues all the same:

Filling the double doors to bathe my eyes,
A final flood of colours will live on
As my mind dies,
Burned by my vision of a world that shone
So brightly at the last, and then was gone.

Balcony Scene

Old as the hills and riddled with ill health,
I talk the talk but cannot walk the walk
Save at the pace of drying paint. My wealth
Of stamina is spent. Think of the hawk,
Nailed to its perch by lack of strength, that learns
To sing the lark's song. What else can it do,
While dreaming of the day its power returns?
It is with all my heart I write to you.

My heart alone is what it always was.
The ultrasound shows nothing wrong with it,
And if we smile at that, then it's because
We both know that its physical remit
Was only half the task the poor thing faced.
My heart had spiritual duties too,
And failed at all of them. Worse than a waste
Was how I hurt myself through hurting you.

Or so he says, you think. I know your fear
That my repentance comes too easily.
But to discuss this, let me lure you here,
To sit with me on my stone balcony.
A hint of winter cools the air, but still
It shines like summer. Here I can renew
My wooing, as a cunning stranger will.
His role reversed, your suitor waits for you.

The maple tree, the autumn crocuses –
They think it's spring, and that their lives are long –
Lend colour to the green and grey. This is
A setting too fine for a life gone wrong.
It needs your laughter. Let me do my best
To earn that much, though you not find me true,
Or good, or fair, or fit for any test.
You think that I don't know my debt to you?

High overhead, a pair of swallows fly,
Programmed for Africa, but just for now
They seem sent solely to enchant the eye
Here in this refuge I acquired somehow
Beyond my merit. Now a sudden wave
Of extra sunlight sharpens all the view.
There is a man here you might care to save
From too much solitude. He calls for you.

Here two opposing forces will collide –
Your proper anger and my shamed regret –
With all the weight of justice on your side.
But once we gladly spoke and still might yet.
Come, then, and do not hesitate to say
Art thou not Romeo, and a Montague?
Be wary, but don't brush these words away,
For they are all yours. I wrote this for you.

Sunset Hails a Rising

O lente, lente currite noctis equi!
    – Marlowe, after Ovid

La mer, la mer, toujours recommencée.
    – Valéry

Dying by inches, I can hear the sound
Of all the fine words for the flow of things
The poets and philosophers have used
To mark the path into the killing ground.
Perhaps their one aim was to give words wings,
Or even just to keep themselves amused,
With no thought that they might not be around
To see the rising sun:
But still they found a measure for our plight
As we prepare to leave the world of men.
Run slowly, slowly, horses of the night.
The sea, the sea, always begun again.

In English of due tact, the great lines gain
More than they lose. The grandeur that they keep
From being born in other tongues than ours
Suggests we will have time to taste the rain
As we are drawn into the dreamless sleep
That lasts so long. No supernatural powers
Need be invoked by us to help explain
How we will see the world
Dissolve into the mutability
That feeds the future with our fading past:
The sea, the always self-renewing sea.
The horses of the night that run so fast.

A Note on the Text

In the poem 'Only the Immortal Need Apply', the scene at the Russian Ballet (*Tableau! Scandale!* as the central figure might have said) is taken from Lucy Hughes-Hallett's biography of Gabriele d'Annunzio, *The Pike*.

The title of 'Sunset Hails a Rising' started life as a line in a poem by Francis Webb, an Australian poet of the previous generation who spent much of his life as a mental patient. His poems rarely cohered but some of them contained fragments too beautiful to forget. In the same poem, the line from *Doctor Faustus* about the horses of the night was taken from Ovid by Marlowe, who left it in the Latin, changing only the word order. The line from Valéry can be found in *Le Cimitière Marin*, best translated by Derek Mahon; although the two translations here, like the two translations from Marlowe's Latin, are both my own.

In 'Mysterious Arrival of the Dew' every line of the first stanza, with the addition of only a single word, is a *trouvaille* taken from a single paragraph of one of Patrick O'Brian's later novels in the Jack Aubrey sequence.

When I was young, the name of the Sydney suburb Tempe was so closely associated with industrial waste that I later thought Keats was joking when he used the name Tempe as short-hand for Arcadia. Later still, while I was living in England, Tempe Dump disappeared among the new constructions for the railway approach to Sydney airport. *Sic transit gloria mundi.*

The two separate mentions of Ava Gardner are a coincidence, although I should confess that when I was twelve years old her appearance in *Pandora and the Flying Dutchman* marked me for life, and that I was forever afterwards the Dutchman, played by James Mason as the commander of a ghost ship who was given to reciting quatrains from the Fitzgerald translation of *The Rubaiyat of Omar Khayyam* while he sailed in perpetual search of the woman who would redeem him from his anguish. Later on, when I met my future wife, it turned out that she was in perpetual search of James Mason.

The title of *Compendium Catullianum* was devised for me by Mary Beard in collaboration with Dr Rupert Thompson, the Orator of Cambridge University.

The dedicatory epigraph is my own translation of a fragment from Rilke.